Old BIGGAR
by
Ann Matheson

The Jubilee Fountain (1887), built to celebrate 50 years of Victoria's reign, was one of Biggar's best known landmarks until 1947. For several centuries this wide area of the High Street was the focal point of the town. Here stood the Cross Knowe , a small hill about seven metres high, topped by the market cross which marked the gathering point for the market and where acts were read and proclamations made. Farther east was the Tron Knowe (public weighing place). The Cross Knowe was the site of great revelry in frosty weather when locals would participate in a pastime known as 'Hurley-hacket', a kind of congo on ice which was apparently executed with great style from the top of the knowe to the other side of the street. The market cross, dated 1632 and inscribed with the initials *J.E.W.* (John, Earl of Wigton) 1694, was damaged in the mid-nineteenth century and built into the back wall of the Corn Exchange. Its loss, with that of 'the auld corse knowe' was much lamented by locals and recorded by several local rhymers.

BIBLIOGRAPHY

William Hunter, *Biggar and the House of Fleming*, 1862
W.S. Crocket, *Biggar: Historical, Traditional, Descriptive Biggar Official Guide*
Rev W.G. Duncan, *Guide to the Town of Biggar*, 1920
James P. Herriot, *History of Biggar Bowling Club, 1848-1948*
Press cuttings, *Dalkeith Advertiser*, May 1906
Biggar Public Park and Golf Club Bazaar
Sir John Sinclair, *Statistical Account of Scotland Vol. 1*, 1791-1799
New Statistical Account of Lanarkshire, 1841
George Thomson, *Third Statistical Account of Scotland – The County of Lanark*, 1960
Biggar Golf Club Minutes, Vol. 1, 1895-1900
Rev. David S. Rutherford, *Biggar St Mary's Medieval College Kirk*
James Alexander Wilson, *A Contribution to the History of Lanarkshire*, 1937
G.V. Irvine and A. Murray, *The Upper Wards of Lanarkshire*, Vol. 1

ACKNOWLEDGEMENTS

Brian Lambie, Biggar Museum Trust, Alasdair Anderson, Angus Matheson. With the exception of those on pages 9, 11, 17, 18, 22, 32, 43 and 48, all pictures are reproduced by courtesy of Biggar Museum Trust.

Text © Ann Matheson 1998
First published in the United Kingdom, 1998
by Stenlake Publishing Ltd.
01290 551122
www.stenlake.co.uk
ISBN 978-1-84033-574-3

Printed by
Blissetts, Roslin Road, Acton, W3 8DH

Will Bulloch, known as 'Stumpy' for obvious, if politically incorrect reasons, was one of the last weavers in Biggar. He augmented his weaver's pittance which, by the 1880s, was barely above subsistence level, by his other trade of bill sticking. Stumpy lived in one of the Gasworks cottages in the Burn Braes.

Introduction

Overlooking Biggar to the north is the spiny ridge of Bizzyberry Hill. Although Stone and Bronze Age remains have been found in the district, this hill, like many others in the area, has evidence of actual settlement dating back almost 2,000 years to the Iron Age. In those times, the Biggar Gap, the broad, flat breach that links the upper Clyde and Tweed valleys, would have been marshy, frequently flooded and heavily wooded, so that the rounded hill-tops flanking it provided excellent dry, defensive sites for Iron Age settlers. These hill-tops were further fortified by concentric rings of ramparts and ditches, many of which still remain.

The town is sited just above the valley floor where conditions would have been drier – but where water was available from the Biggar Water which flows south through the western part of the town then eastwards along the Biggar Gap to join the Tweed. Biggar's location in this gap, where east-west routes meet the north-south routes from the Clyde and Tweed valleys, has always been important to its development as a centre of trade and commerce. Biggar was also an ecclesiastical centre, the ancient church of Saint Nicholas preceding the later St Mary's on the same site.

The etymology of the name Biggar is impossible to resolve. Several suggestions have been made, including 'barley land' and 'soft land', but perhaps, in view of Biggar's location only a mile from a 90° bend in the Clyde the most plausible is the derivation from the Anglo-Saxon big or bige, meaning 'bend'.

In the twelfth century, following the Norman Conquest in England, many Normans infiltrated into Scotland. In return for the promise of military support, King David I gave the lands of Biggar to Baldwin, a Fleming leader. These Flemings, a branch of the Normans, built their stronghold in Biggar where the remains of their motte and bailey castle can still be seen north-west of the High Street, overlooking the Burn Braes.

The Flemings continued to be the town's overlords, moving probably in the early 16th century to Boghall Castle. With several hundred yards of bog behind it, the castle was easily defended from the rear and fortified in front by a 30 foot wall with gun towers as well as a surrounding ditch. It fell into ruin in the eighteenth century after the death of the last Earl of Wigton, when it became the property of the Elphinstone family who were not concerned about its preservation. The Flemings supported Bruce in his bid for the Scottish crown. Legend reports that, when Bruce murdered his rival, Comyn, in the Church of the Greyfriars at Dumfries, Robert Fleming of Biggar and his supporters, who went to verify the deed, cut off Comyn's head and raised it aloft, crying 'let the deed shaw'. This was adopted as the motto on the crest of the Flemings of Biggar.

During the Middle Ages, Biggar continued to develop as a route centre and market town. In 1451, King James II made Biggar a free Burgh of Barony, giving the town the right to hold a weekly market, annual fairs and the powers of jurisdiction and custom levy. To this day, the town centre retains the medieval layout of broad High Street, where the market stalls would have been set up, and, parallel to this, the narrow North and South Back Roads, linked to the main street by closes and loans (lanes). With annual fairs for hiring and stock and seed sales, Biggar flourished. Local industries developed, typical of market towns and based on agricultural raw materials. By the early eighteenth century, the town supported over 200 handloom weavers and numerous tailors, wrights, shoemakers and blacksmiths. The Burn Braes became a mini industrial axis where the grain mill, wauking and dyeing works and brewery made use of the adjacent water supply. Along the terrace above the valley, a row of substantial weavers' houses provided both home and workplace for their residents. Up to the mid-nineteenth century, these Westraw folk formed a separate community, with their own societies and birlemen. The town was also a focal point for carriers and the depot for Leadhills lead which was carted to Biggar before being despatched to Leith. Far from being parochial, Biggar was a staging point for carriers from the south and west en route to Edinburgh. In Biggar and the House of Fleming, W. Hunter records that the High Street was continually in a stir as a constant succession of carriers arrived, often accompanied by packs of yapping dogs. Economic prosperity and civic confidence are reflected in the fine nineteenth century buildings like the Corn Exchange, the South Public and Parish Schools, the auction mart and no less than three banks.

The late nineteenth century saw great changes in the town's economic structure. The 1861 census records only 60 weavers, their trade destroyed by cheaper mass-produced goods from the coal-driven factories of the Industrial Revolution. The coming of the railways and the building of the auction market in 1874 brought an end to the colourful fairs and street markets of the past. The railway link, however, also resulted in the arrival of the first commuters, who built handsome villas at both ends of the town – and the start of the tourist industry. By the mid-twentieth century, Biggar had become a popular destination for day-trippers from Glasgow and Edinburgh, now only a short drive away.

Today, small local industries recall the traditional ones – weaving, food processing and agricultural machinery: but with a difference. The new industries are highly specialised, enabling them to reach a world, rather than a local market. Most of the town's workers are, however, employed in the tertiary sector, providing services for both tourists and a large local hinterland. Biggar Museum Trust is perhaps the best known of all these local industries, managing to service six museums with a tiny staff and 5% of the population as volunteer labour. The town has been described as a 'metropolitan village', because it offers to both residents and visitors many more specialised services than one would normally expect to find in a settlement of just over 2,000 people.

Informed civic policy has ensured that all new developments are carefully monitored. Much of the town is conservation area with almost a hundred listed buildings, and any new development must meet the stringent criteria of the planning committees. While it is unlikely that Biggar will change much in the foreseeable future, it is always chancy to rely too much on a fluctuating tourist trade and many residents would be glad to see the controlled development of small-scale industry to provide a more stable economic base.

In 1737, many Scottish churchgoers who refused to condone undue state interference in the Established Kirk, left to join the Secession Church founded by Ebenezer Erskine in 1733. For about fifteen years, the Biggar Seceders attended the Secession Church at West Linton until they were able to build their own place of worship on the north side of the High Street in 1760. The church in the picture is the Burgher Kirk, which was built on the site of the original Secession Kirk in 1806. This building was converted into houses when the Moat Park Church, now the hub of Biggar Museum Trust, was built in 1865.

This grand wedding – the marriage of J.M. Cairns to Mary G. Murray of Spittal – took place in St Mary's Church, now known as Biggar Kirk, in 1914. This is the site of the much older Church of St Nicholas, first mentioned in church records between 1165 and 1170, where it is recorded that Robert, the parson of Biggar, witnessed a grant of meal to the monks of Paisley Abbey. In 1545 Malcolm, Lord Fleming, founded a Collegiate Church on the site. This church was to support a provost, eight canons or prebendaries, four singing boys and six poor men called beidsmen. The prebendaries, in addition to their ecclesiastical duties, were responsible for the education of the boys as well as the care of the beidsmen. In turn, the beidsmen had to sit by the graves of the founder and his descendants and pray for the Fleming souls, in return for which they received annually a white linen gown and hood. John Tweedie of Drumelzier contributed an annual endowment of £10 for masses to be said for the soul of the founder's father, John, Lord Fleming, whom he had murdered. The remains of jougs, where wrongdoers were chained to atone for their misdeeds, can be seen at the south transept door. As a collegiate church, Biggar Kirk was short-lived since the Scottish church became Protestant after the Reformation of 1560.

The piece of land on which this church fair is taking place has seen many changes. The wooded flat-topped mound in the background is a twelfth century Norman motte. On this defensive site, where they could see their enemies approach, the earliest Flemings built the castle which they occupied for several centuries. The motte overlooks the Burn Braes area which, in the Middle Ages, would have been very marshy and difficult for enemies to penetrate. The flat lawn in the foreground of the picture was created in 1848 to make a town bowling green. This area would have been part of the bailey, enclosed by a high wooden palisade, where soldiers were garrisoned. The picture shows what is now the Biggar Kirk manse lawn.

Since the Biggar Burn was too sluggish to turn a mill wheel, the artificial channel or lade (above) was cut to bring water from higher up the valley. The mill, which ground meal and malt, and Rowhead Farm opposite it, were the property of the Free Church. Rents from these provided four scholarships in the New College, Edinburgh. In the background are both Biggar Kirk and the spire of the Gillespie Church. The unpopular Patronage Act, which gave landowners the sole right to appoint ministers, had resulted in the founding of the Relief Church by Thomas Gillespie in 1751. The appointment of an unpopular Biggar minister led to members of the Biggar congregation joining the Dissenters in 1779. Their Relief Church later became the South UP Church which was in turn replaced by the Gillespie Church, named after Thomas Gillespie, in 1878. Biggar congregations seem to have been very determined folk. John Reid, like many ministers in Scotland, was the victim of both the government, who tried to reintroduce bishops, and the congregation, who stripped him of his charge or 'rabbled' him when he attempted to carry out the government's orders. On another occasion, in 1752, the Moat Park church congregation made pressing representations against the appointment of William Haig whose voice and constitution were both apparently too feeble for their requirements! In 1662, when Charles II passed Acts of Parliament to restore bishops and the right of patronage, all twelve ministers of Biggar Presbytery resigned; four of them were later imprisoned on the Bass Rock.

William Aitchison, local carter, poses outside 45 High Street with a cart-load of meal from the mill. The photograph dates from *c*.1904 and was taken from the doorway of the photographic studio directly opposite. At the time, the property in the background was a single storey house.

The meandering Biggar Burn was used by local residents for washing and bleaching their clothes. When the tenant of Rowhead Farm straightened the burn in 1863, the locals quickly undid the work, resulting in a summons to Lanark Sheriff Court where their plea of 'use and wont' fell on deaf ears. In the seventeenth century, a wauk mill and dyeing works made use of the ready water supply, while the lower slopes of the motte were known as the Preaching Braes, where outdoor meetings, both religious and secular, took place. The level land below this, where sports were held in June, was known as Angus's Green.

Up to the 1890s, censuses show that there were about 25-30 shoemakers in the town, one of whom was John Rae, who lived from 1843 until 1933. His shoemaking was carried out in the back shop of what is now 169 High Street where, according to a story written by his son Gilbert, the shoemakers sang in harmony as they worked. Pictured also is Jimmy the parrot, who was brought from South Africa by another of John's sons, Andrew. What appears to be a coil of rope is in fact a bee skep. John Rae also set up a nursery business, growing tomatoes which were once known as 'love apples' and eaten sprinkled with sugar.

Members of the Hutcheson family photographed outside their home in the courtyard of the old brewery at the foot of the Wynd, 1909. The courtyard and buildings remain, now largely converted into houses; brewing ceased in the first half of the nineteenth century. At that time, one of the lofts was sometimes used as a theatre by local and visiting groups. The first local production in the brewery loft was Home's *Douglas*, but we have no record of any spectator reacting, as one did at its first performance in Edinburgh in 1756, by shouting enthusiastically, 'Whaur's yer Wullie Shakespeare noo?'.

The ruins of Boghall Castle belie its former importance as the seat of the Flemings, who played an important role in Scottish history throughout the Middle Ages and up to the eighteenth century. James, 4th Lord Fleming, was one of eight commissioners chosen to represent Scotland in 1558 at the marriage of Mary, Queen of Scots to the Dauphin. Their refusal to consent to anything that would alter the succession to the Scottish crown so incensed the French court that poison was, allegedly, administered and three of them died within a few days. Lord Fleming, who was only twenty-four, died some weeks later in Paris. His son also met his death at the hands of the French, but this time inadvertently, when a troop of French soldiers fired off a volley in his honour and the bullets ricocheted off the causeway in Edinburgh, wounding him fatally, if perhaps euphemistically, 'above the knee'. James VI, who went hawking and hunting in Biggar, restored the title 'Earl of Wigton' to the 6th Lord Fleming. During the seventeenth century religious wars, the castle was raided several times and taken by Cromwell in 1651. While successive earls flirted with both sides, the wife of the 4th Earl (1665-1668) was the Covenanting Countess of the famous Boghall conventicles.

One of Biggar's best known and still extant traditions is the Hogmanay bonfire, which is lit around 9.30 p.m. on Hogmanay and usually continues to smoulder for two or three days into the next year. Preparations begin in early December to collect combustible material for this huge fire, which is usually lit by a senior citizen of the burgh following a torch-lit procession from the Cadger's Brig to the bonfire site outside the Corn Exchange. It was an old Biggar custom that men who had this honour flung their bunnets into the fire after the torch. These boys were photographed collecting wood for the bonfire c.1905-06. The Albion in the background, with driver Ally Noble, was the delivery van for Oven's Grocers.

Until the mid-nineteenth century, Westraw residents had their own societies, peat moss, birlemen, and even their own bonfire site, a level grassy platform which can still be seen in the Burn Braes. W.B. Pairman's *Ballads o' Biggar* (1928) records the rivalry of the days when 'us douce Biggar lads used to whummle yon loons o Westraw', as well as the rhythmic working of the loom from the homes of the Westraw hand loom weavers:

Treadle, Beam, Clip-clap,
Hand, Shuttle, Reel
Clipperty-clapperty
Clipperty-clapperty
Clap

Glasgow agents brought in the raw cotton and sold the finished cloth. By the 1850s, however, the weavers could no longer compete with cheaper factory-produced material and started to make woollen cloth or a coarse wool-linen mixture; some knitted stockings. This industry too came to an end and, by the turn of the century, there were no weavers left.

Burnside Terrace (above, right) consisted of back-to-back 'flats' built into the steep valley side of the Biggar Burn. Upper floor residents entered from the road side, while ground floor residents had access from the Burn Braes side. The old man with the hay rake and barrowload of hay is James Plenderleith who died in 1894, aged 91. A letter box now stands on the site of the well where the children are clustered. In 1831 more than half Biggar's workforce consisted of weavers, of which there were 210. Other well-represented professions included shoemakers (28), masons (26), tailors (20), carters (20) and spirit-dealers (16), not to mention the more archaic professions such as the 8 nailers, 2 tinsmiths, and sole umbrella-maker.

The whitewashed Gasworks cottages were demolished just before the Second World War. One of them was a small 'Jenny aa Things' shop with a sign on the wall advertising tea and snuff. Biggar Gasworks, across from the cottages, produced gas for domestic purposes and street lighting from 1839 until 1973, when they were closed following the arrival of North Sea gas. Preserved as they were in 1973, the works are now part of the Biggar Museum Trust complex.

Mid Toftcombs cottage was the home of the Gladstones or, as they were known in earlier times, Gledstanes. William Gledstanes came to Biggar as a maltster in the early eighteenth century. His son John (1693-1756), who settled in this cottage, was the great-grandfather of William Ewart Gladstone who was Prime Minister several times and one of the great nineteenth century Liberal reformers. William Ewart was, however, born in Liverpool where his father, John, had amassed a fortune in the West India trade. In the 1860s the cottage had a major face-lift when the windows were enlarged and the diamond-shaped panes installed. At the door, around 1900, are some of the Sanderson family. By the 1950s, the cottage had fallen into a sad state of disrepair and now scarcely a ruin remains to mark the spot where it stood.

Jackson, Biggar

In 1747 the parish schoolmaster complained to the Bailie that private schools in the town were damaging the prospects of his own. The Bailie upheld his complaint, since an Act had been passed in Biggar in 1722 forbidding any school other than the parish one. At that time children attending school brought a peat to heat the schoolroom with them. In the nineteenth century local schools were largely maintained by endowments left by several local men for the furtherance of education in the burgh. Among these were William Law, who was a skinner, and William Nisbet, a hawker of salt. Funds were raised in 1849 to build a new parish school. Thanks to subscriptions, public collections, concerts and sales of work, as well as a free architectural plan and the loan of horses to transport materials, the new parish school (now the Municipal Hall) was built – but had room for only 180 of the 330 children of school age. Ten years later, the Burgh or South Public School (now Biggar Primary) was built in John's Loan. By 1905, when this picture was taken, the South Public School had become the High School.

18

Taken outside the then High School, now Biggar Primary, these young men are going through their paces in what used to be called 'drill'. Apart from the lamp post and the spiked iron railing in the playground, this scene has changed very little since 1905. In the nineteenth century, the Female Industrial School, now a private house at 9 Mid Road, catered for 'the daughters of the working classes'. Here, in addition to their ordinary education, the girls learned the 'womanly' arts of knitting, sewing and singing.

Both racquets and dress have changed a bit since this photograph was taken at Biggar Park *c.*1884. Public tennis courts were opened in 1885 alongside the bowling green.

In 1874, this green replaced the former bowling green beside the motte. Although the latter had been in regular use since 1848, the overshadowing trees had made it impossible for play to begin until mid-June. To meet the costs of erecting the new club-house in 1881, a share company was formed and the management committee seems to have exercised strict discipline in their financial dealings. Members who failed to pay their subscriptions were issued with a summons from the local solicitor and had their names posted on the club house wall. This picture dates from 1911-12.

In 1895, a 9 hole golf course was opened at Langlees about two miles west of Biggar. This original course had certain problems, mainly that the tenant insisted that his sheep and cattle continue to graze there. Consequently, in 1901, the club members rented a larger piece of land at Heavyside where the greenkeeper, rather than the beasts, kept the grass down. The third and final move took place in 1907 when Biggar Town Council opened the town's new Public Park with 9 hole golf course (above), boating pond and football pitch.

On 17 July 1907, the official opening day of the Public Park, this grand parade of schoolchildren, golfers, folk in fancy dress and council officials took place through the town headed by Dr Guthrie's Juvenile Pipe Band. At the park, the official speeches were made and refreshments served in a large marquee at the side of the new boating pond. The creation of the Public Park reflected the growing importance of Biggar as a holiday centre and health resort in the early twentieth century. In July and August the town was like a fashionable spa resort, with lists of holidaymakers printed every week to enable visitors to make social calls on one another.

Curling on Biggar Pond.

This photograph was taken *c.*1905 when outdoor curling was taken for granted as a regular winter sport. The makeshift curling pond here, now part of the Public Park, was simply floodwater. Marked on the 1859 map of the town is the main curling pond at the extreme eastern end of Mid Road in the boggy south-western corner of Biggar Moss. In those days, most of the surrounding villages had similar ponds and competition between teams was intense.

The boating pond is one of the main attractions of the park. The old golf pavilion came from the Heavyside course outside Biggar and the shop was brought from Talla where it had served as a hospital for the navvies who were building the reservoir.

A·I·Y· CAMP · BIGGAR · 1910 ·

The Ayrshire Imperial Yeomanry, camped on the field which is now the site of Boghall housing estate. This picture was taken in 1910 when yeomanry and volunteer camps were a popular recreation and a regular feature of rural areas.

Six years later, war was for real. This cartload of wartime supplies was *en route* to Biggar Station *c.*1916. The station carter, with the stylish bowler hat, is 'Bowff' Graham; Bert Aitchison, son of the contractor William Aitchison, is beside the horse. The poster on the cart, copies of which were posted throughout the country, read 'Will you send us some apples, oranges and fresh vegetables etc. FOR THE FLEET'.

Haldane and Tait, coachbuilders, had their premises in the South Back Road (now Siller Knowe Court). Standing at the front of this elegant coach is James Gibson who was killed in the First World War.

Willie Marshall, W.B. Stephen, Jimmy Gibson and Malcolm McColl take a break outside W.B. Stephen's garage in the High Street. The building's stonework is of a very traditional style. Much of the local stone is plum whinstone, a very hard rock which is difficult, and therefore very expensive, to cut into regular blocks. Consequently, most buildings have dressed stone in front with random work at the sides and rear. Before becoming a garage, this building was a smiddy.

The first sod of the Symington, Biggar and Broughton branch of the Caledonian Railway was cut on 30 September 1858, and several stretches of Roman road were uncovered when the track was being laid. The railway's opening in 1860 led to changed fortunes in the town, facilitating commuting and encouraging tourism, but also spelling loss to the numerous carriers, innkeepers and stablers whose livelihoods depended on the horse-drawn carriage. Of particular significance was the loss of the lead trade. Before the coming of the railway around 900 cartloads (800 tons) of lead a year had passed through Biggar on its journey from Leadhills to Leith. A distinguishing feature of the High Street had been the piles of lead bars waiting to be uplifted by the carriers. This picture was taken c.1900 by Dr Tom Pairman on a visit home from New Zealand.

Back row, left to right: Alex Thorburn junior, Sanny Ramsay, Alex Brownlie, John Linn, Walter Campbell. Kneeling left: George Inverarity. Kneeling right: unknown. The station master is Alex Thorburn and seated in front is Alex Stephen who later went on to wear the station master's lum hat in Central Station, Glasgow. The photograph was taken in the early 1920s.

Looking up the High Street from the west end of town. The three storied Victoria buildings would have been only a few years old when this picture was taken in the early 1900s. The architect was William Brown of Paisley and the style reminiscent of some of the art nouveau work of the West of Scotland at that time. Right of the butchers is the building which had been the post office until 1898 and, on its left, Gilbert Rae's ironmongery store, shown close-up on the opposite page.

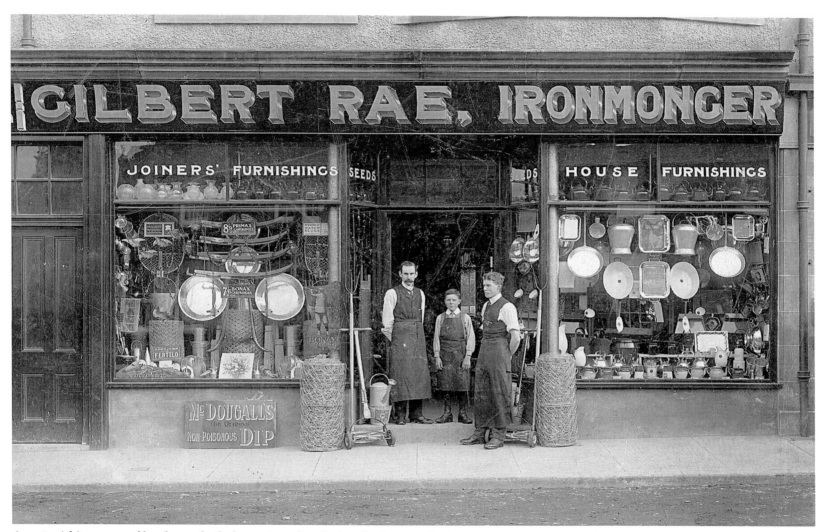

An astonishing array of hardware, both domestic and agricultural, photographed *c.*1909. Pictured *right to left* are John Rae, brother of the proprietor, Hubert Don and Gilbert Rae who, as well as being the shop owner, was a well known local vernacular poet and writer.

R. Thomson (left), Jim McCann and W. Aitken pose outside the Fleming Arms with a mountain of bottles collected for Biggar's Bottle Drive during the First World War. Both wars saw national efforts like this to gather reusable objects and help combat shortages of raw materials.

Four young assistants of John Gladstone, Ironmonger, photographed in 1889. Left to right are Tom Plenderleith, John Newbigging, Tom Ballantyne and a boyish Gilbert Rae. The shop was at 119 High Street and their store at 113B High Street in what is now Brian's Yard.

This convoy, on its way to the Ministry of Supply in London from the Albion works in Glasgow, visited Biggar in 1915. Standing alongside the leading vehicle is the Blackwood Murray family. In 1899, Dr Blackwood Murray of Heavyside, Biggar, and his brother-in-law, Norman Fulton, founded the Albion Motor Company. During the First World War, production switched to army transport vehicles and this is a group of the famous A10s which were destined for service in France. Over 6,000 of these vehicles were produced during the First World War. Albion enthusiasts from all over the world are in regular contact with Biggar's Albion archive, and the annual Biggar rally is a must for veteran and vintage car owners all over Britain.

The poet Hugh MacDiarmid (Christopher Murray Grieve) lived at Brownsbank Cottage, about two miles from Biggar, from 1951 until his death in 1978. This picture, taken in 1968, shows him opening Biggar's first museum, the Victorian Gladstone Court. Looking on is a youthful Brian Lambie, the man responsible for Biggar's museum industry. Little did MacDiarmid know that twenty-one years later, after the death of his wife Valda, his own home, Brownsbank Cottage, would also become one of Biggar's museums! While Gladstone Court has since been extended and is now one of six museums run by Biggar Museum Trust, Brownsbank Cottage, preserved with most of its artefacts, functions as a base for a writer-in-residence.

GERMAN GIPSY ENCAMPMENT. BIGGAR. AUG. 1906.

Local residents gather at the Burn Braes for a glimpse of the exotic. German gypsies, perhaps driven from their homeland by increased taxation on horse trading, camped here in August 1906. They were probably a contingent of the same group who camped in the Dalkeith/Gorebridge district in May of that year, having landed in Hartlepool and worked their way north. Some local people felt uneasy about their presence, since the gypsies, who did not deal in regular currency and didn't speak English, could be very persuasive in their attempts at barter! The *Dalkeith Advertiser* of 31 May 1906 describes the mixture of avid curiosity and fear with which they were greeted. Locals were particularly disturbed by the aggressive begging of the women and children and the 'cool audacity' with which the men entered private houses. When the gypsies refused adamantly to be photographed unless they were paid, a young Biggar man, John George Brown, took several illicit photographs with a camera hidden inside his coat. Despite official papers which stated they were dealers in pots and pans, there was no evidence of this type of trading and they were consequently suspected of being spies. *Biggar Museum Trust would be most interested to hear from anyone with any more information about the gypsies.*

Perhaps even more exotic is the sight of these beasts from Bostock and Wombell's Circus wandering about Biggar High Street on an October day in 1908. This circus regularly visited Biggar, arriving by road and special train. Local children were particularly attracted to the High Street parade . . . maybe because it was free!

This picture recalls the days, not so far distant, when every town had its own bakery. When Wm. Gibson built these dazzling new premises in 1953-54, the bakehouse was opened to the public for a few days. The large circular machine centre-stage was a dough mixer which mixed 400 loaves at a time. Bill Sharp, extreme right, remembers making pancakes for three days to entertain the visitors. Others pictured are (left to right) Jimmy Reid, Forrest Vance, J. Thomson Gibson, Bing Anderson, Robert Mitchell and a young woman whose identity is unknown. In these pre-supermarket days, a fleet of vans delivered the produce to the local area, but the bakery's heyday was short-lived. It was purchased by Rank-Hovis and all this sparkling machinery transferred to Edinburgh.

Admiring their preparations for this exquisite Christmas Buffet in the 1930s in Wilson's Hall are (left to right): Jen Wilson (Mrs Bryden), Mrs Wilson, Mrs George Wilson, Nan Forrest (Mrs Mitchell) and Maisie Ramsay.

Secondary education 1903-style, when lace collars were the ultimate fashion accessory. Standing by the blackboard are Bessie Gladstone (right) and an unknown classmate. Others (left to right) are Annie Hoatson, Nan Brunton, Kate Sked, Meg Sibbald, Annie Davidson, Anna Paterson, Min Weir, Lily Prentice and Dora Don. Mr Rodgers is beside the chemical cupboard and the three boys (left to right) are John Brown, Mungo Aitken and Bert Harris. Two of these young scientists, Bessie Gladstone and Bert Harris, later married one another and after a career at the RAE Farnborough, Bert became Professor of Aeronautics at Bangalore University. Min Weir died in 1988, having reached the grand age of 101 (and a half!)

Biggar High School pupils respond to the appeal on the poster, seen in the picture of the carter on page 27. Their Merry Christmas to the Fleet takes the form of all kinds of goodies from shortbread and stock cubes to mystery parcels, cloutie dumplings and piles of shiny apples. From left to right, the pupil organisers are Mary Harper, Madeline Brunton, Katie Thorburn, Eppie Colthart, Emily Thorburn, Lina Clarkson, Sarah Thomson, Sybil Ferguson, Annie Plenderleith, Jessie Meiklem, Annie Wilson and Amy Don.

These nurses are members of the Voluntary Aid Detachment (VAD), part of the Red Cross movement, on duty at Biggar Agricultural Show in 1919. Only some of the nurses can be identified. Back row: Ailie Forrest (fourth from left), Mrs Edmund Hope (second from right); seated: Joan Summerville (left) and Tilda Higgins (second from right). The lad in front with the goat is R.G. Murray of Spittal. A white goat with gold horns is the crest of the Fleming family. No one knows why the goat was adopted, but it may have entered the Fleming coat of arms following a marriage with the Frasers in the early 1300s. When James Shepherd, headmaster of Biggar High School from 1956 to 1972, applied to the Lord Lyon for accreditation of a school badge, he was dismayed to discover that the goat had to be included. This he considered an unfortunate and inappropriate symbol for an educational establishment and thereafter he always referred to it as 'that animal'!

Ena Kay, Fleming Queen, poses with the lads before the match, 1930. Since there are several Symington players in the photograph, this was probably a local derby game that was part of the Gala week festivities.

Since 1929, when this picture was taken, the crowning of the Fleming Queen has been the high point of Biggar's Gala Day, which commemorates the occasion when Mary Fleming of Boghall Castle was made Queen of the Epiphany Revels at Holyrood Palace in 1563. Mary Fleming, allegedly the Queen's favourite, was the only attendant at Mary's secret marriage to Darnley. When the Lords of the Congregation objected to this marriage and rallied an army against her, Mary in turn mobilised her supporters in Biggar where 18,000 men awaited her when she arrived at Boghall with Darnley to command her troops. Five years later, after her defeat at the Battle of Langside, the Regent Moray besieged and partly demolished Boghall Castle and several other buildings in the town. Here, at the war memorial, crowds await the arrival of the Fleming Queen. The memorial design is based on the market cross which stood in the middle of the High Street. The lone figure with the camera stand, left of the memorial, is Jimmy Jamieson, the official photographer, unaware that he too was being snapped by a press photographer who took this one from Victoria Buildings.

The Roman charioteer, rounding the corner at Kirkstyle in the 1930 Gala Day, recalls an earlier period of history when Biggar would have been a stopping point between two important Roman camps at Carstairs and Lyne, near Peebles. Several relics from this period are on display in Moat Park Heritage Centre.

Blind Harry's *Life of Wallace* claims that the Scots, under Wallace, won a great victory over the English, commanded by Edward I, at Biggar. Hearing that Wallace had raised the standard of independence at Lanark, Edward marched into Scotland with 60,000 men. From their camp at Biggar, he sent messengers to Wallace, camped on Tinto Hill, that surrender would earn him a pardon: otherwise, he would be treated as a rebel. Wallace, treating this message with contempt, dealt cruelly with the heralds, putting out the eyes of one and cutting off the other's tongue. Disguised as a cadger (hawker), Wallace allegedly went to spy out the enemy camp and was pursued back into Biggar where he stoutly defended himself at 'Cadger's Brig'. Joined by a party from Annandale, the Scottish forces were able to defeat Edward's army. But Blind Harry's poem is inconsistent with historical documents. It is true, however, that in 1302 the Scottish forces assembled at Biggar marched from there to the Battle of Roslin, managing to rout the first division of the English army in the early dawn. Since Blind Harry's poem describes identical battle sequences to those of the Battle of Roslin, perhaps he simply relocated that battle in Biggar – although neither Wallace nor Edward were present at the Battle of Roslin, despite subsequent English historians claiming that they were! Whatever the truth, Wallace is the undoubted hero of the centuries-old Biggar *Seguiser* play.